NATIONAL GEOGRAPHIC

T0288456

Race Around the WORLD

PIONEER EDITION

By Brian LaFleur and Beth Geiger

CONTENTS

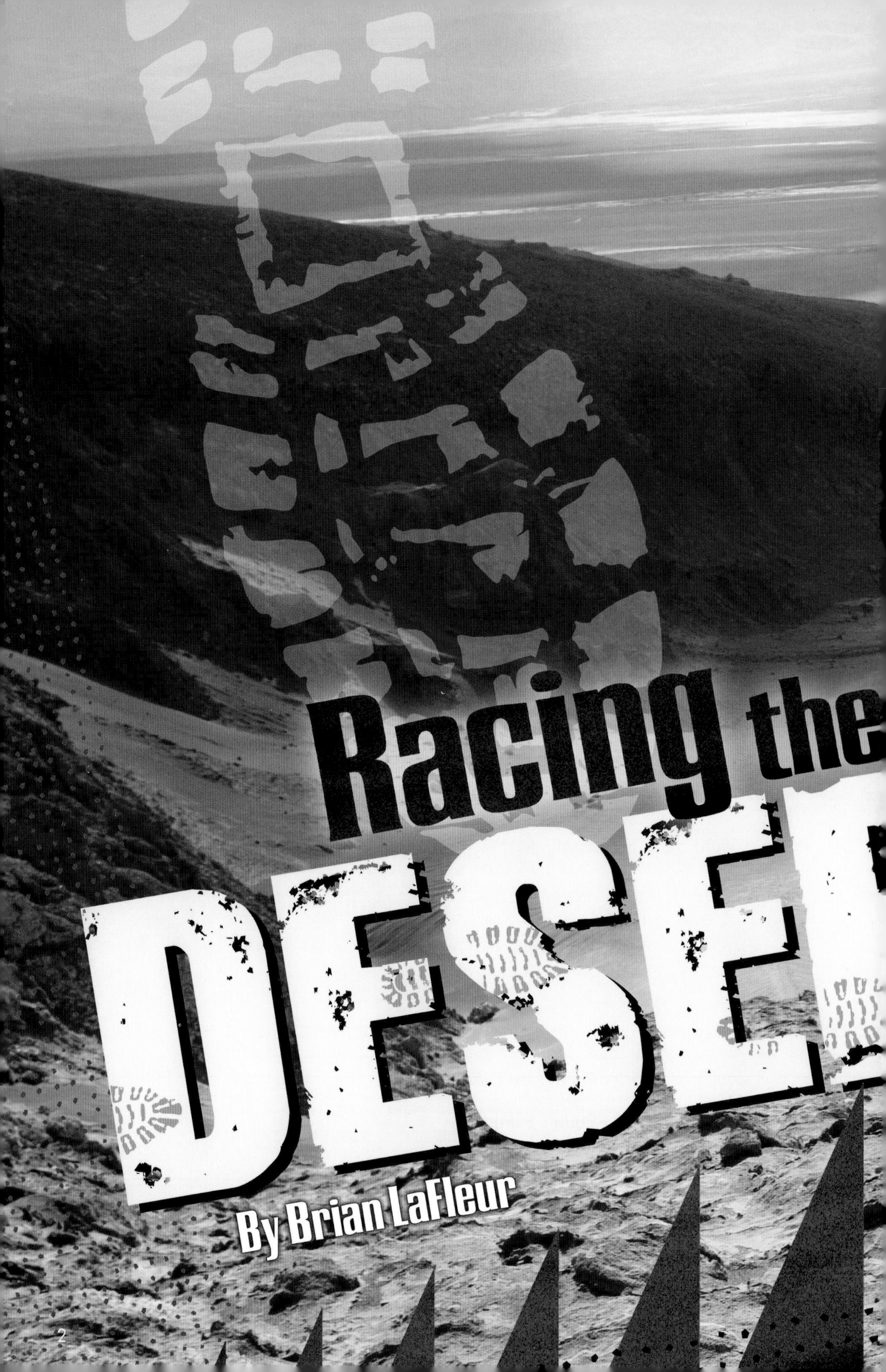

Racing the DESE

By Brian LaFleur

Would you like to race across a very hot desert? You'll carry food and clothes on your back. You'll be exhausted. You'll collapse in a tent at night. You'll wake up the next morning and do it all over again!

Tough runners race through deserts every year. These racers will tell you it's miserable. But they love the challenge.

The runners race across the **harshest** places on Earth. It's all part of the Four Deserts Race.

This is no ordinary race. The race has four parts. Each part takes place in a different desert. The four deserts are the Atacama, Gobi, Sahara, and Antarctica. Racers run through the driest and hottest places on Earth. They run through the coldest and windiest places, too!

Each of the parts is 250 kilometers (155 miles) long. Racers must run it in six days. Is this race for you? Here's what you need to know.

Harsh Place. *An Italian racer runs across the Atacama Desert in Chile, South America.*

Desert Data

You need to know a little about deserts before you begin the race. Deserts are on every continent. They all have one thing in common. They are dry. Deserts get less than 25 centimeters (10 inches) of rain or snow per year.

That's where the similarities end. Some deserts are hot and sandy. Others are cold and rocky. Some are flat. Others have mountains. Each is different. So each desert has its own challenges for the racers. You'll be hot one week. You'll be cold the next. You'll climb mountains. You'll trudge through sand.

The Dry Atacama

Now you know about deserts. Let the race begin!

You fly to South America in March. The Atacama in Chile is the first desert in the race. It is also the driest place on Earth. Some parts of the Atacama desert have never had even one drop of water!

Your training can't prepare you for the salt plains. One racer said it was like "stepping on millions of pieces of broken glass, uneven pebbles, and hard rocks at the same time."

You cross the finish line. But, you still have three more deserts to go!

Four Deserts Race Locations

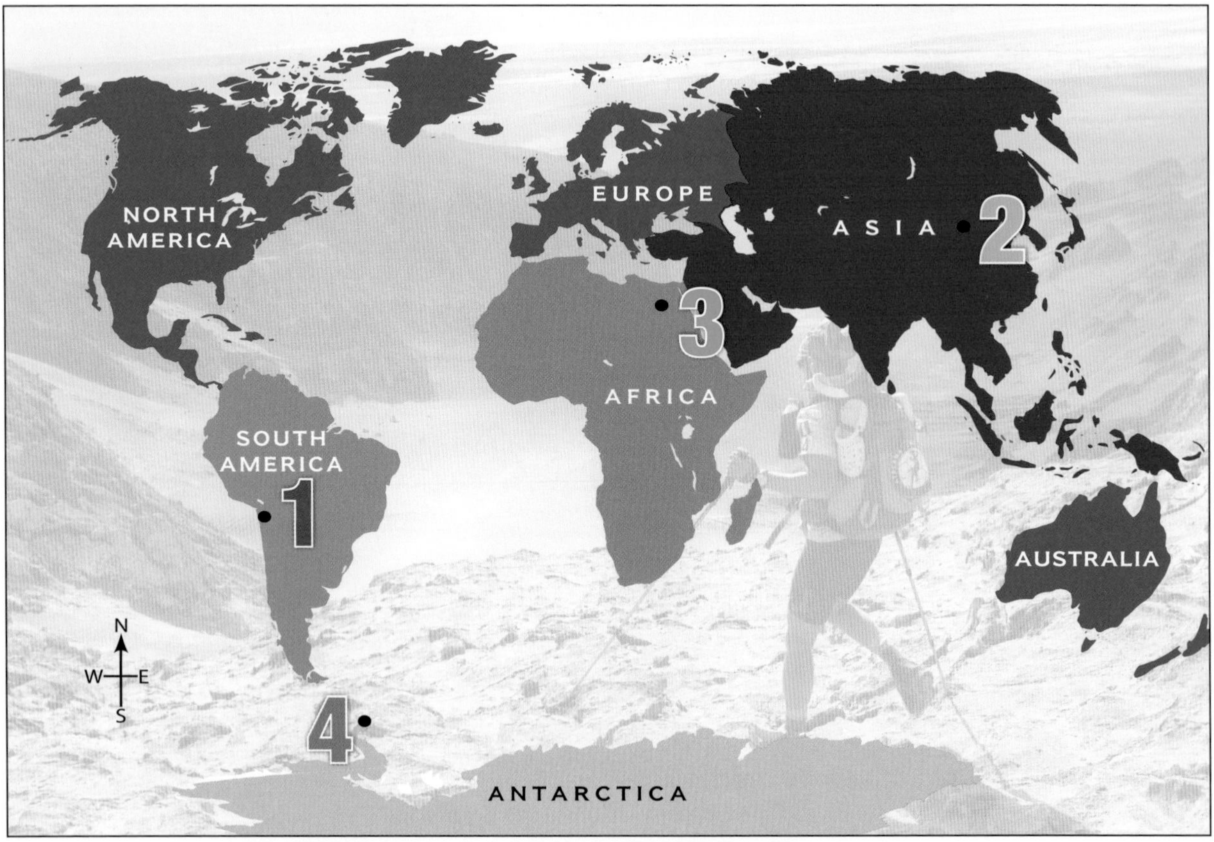

Driest Desert. *Llamas rest in the Atacama Desert.*

Extreme Gobi

It's time to race again in June! You fly to China to tackle the Gobi. It has some sandy areas. But most of the Gobi is rocky.

It is tough to pack for this part. The Gobi is a place of **extremes**. There are burning hot days. But the nights are freezing cold. It is summertime. But in the mountains you face strong winds. There might even be snow. Pack layers of clothes. You can put them on and take them off as the temperature changes.

Keep moving! You are almost halfway done with the race.

Camel Traffic. *Camels have carried people and goods across the Gobi in China for centuries.*

Strong Wind. *Wind carved the rock and blew the sand around this area of the Sahara in Egypt.*

The Singing Sahara

You travel to the Sahara in North Africa in October. It is the hottest place on Earth. It is also Earth's biggest hot desert. The Sahara has lots of sand. Fierce winds blow the sand around in strong sandstorms. Racers have to cover their faces to breathe.

But the sand makes a beautiful sound. It's called singing sand. It can sound like a squeal, a hum, or a roar. Not all deserts have singing sands. Luckily, you're racing through one that does! Once you cross the Sahara, what's next?

Icy Antarctica

The last part of the race might be the hardest part. Antarctica is next. That's right. Antarctica is a desert!

It's the coldest and windiest place on Earth. Parts of this continent get less than five centimeters (two inches) of moisture per year. Not much snow falls. But it piles up for centuries in the extreme cold. Winds here can reach speeds of 300 kilometers (186 miles) per hour.

You move through knee-deep snow. Try to forget how tired your body is, and keep going!

End in Sight

Your **efforts** have paid off. The end of the race is in sight! You cross the finish line in Antarctica. Congratulations! The Four Deserts Race is over.

You think about the amazing things you saw. You forget all your aches, blisters, and sunburns.

These deserts may be the harshest places on Earth, but they are also some of the most beautiful.

Almost There. *Congratulations! You finished the third race! One more to go!*

Wordwise

effort: hard work to do something

extreme: a very great degree of something

harsh: hard and unpleasant

tough: strong and determined; difficult to do

Ice Cold. *Antarctica is the Earth's coldest continent. It surrounds the South Pole.*

EARTH'S EXTREMES

By Beth Geiger

Earth is full of extremes. And you can explore them! Climb the highest peak. Sail along the greatest river. And shiver on the coldest continent.

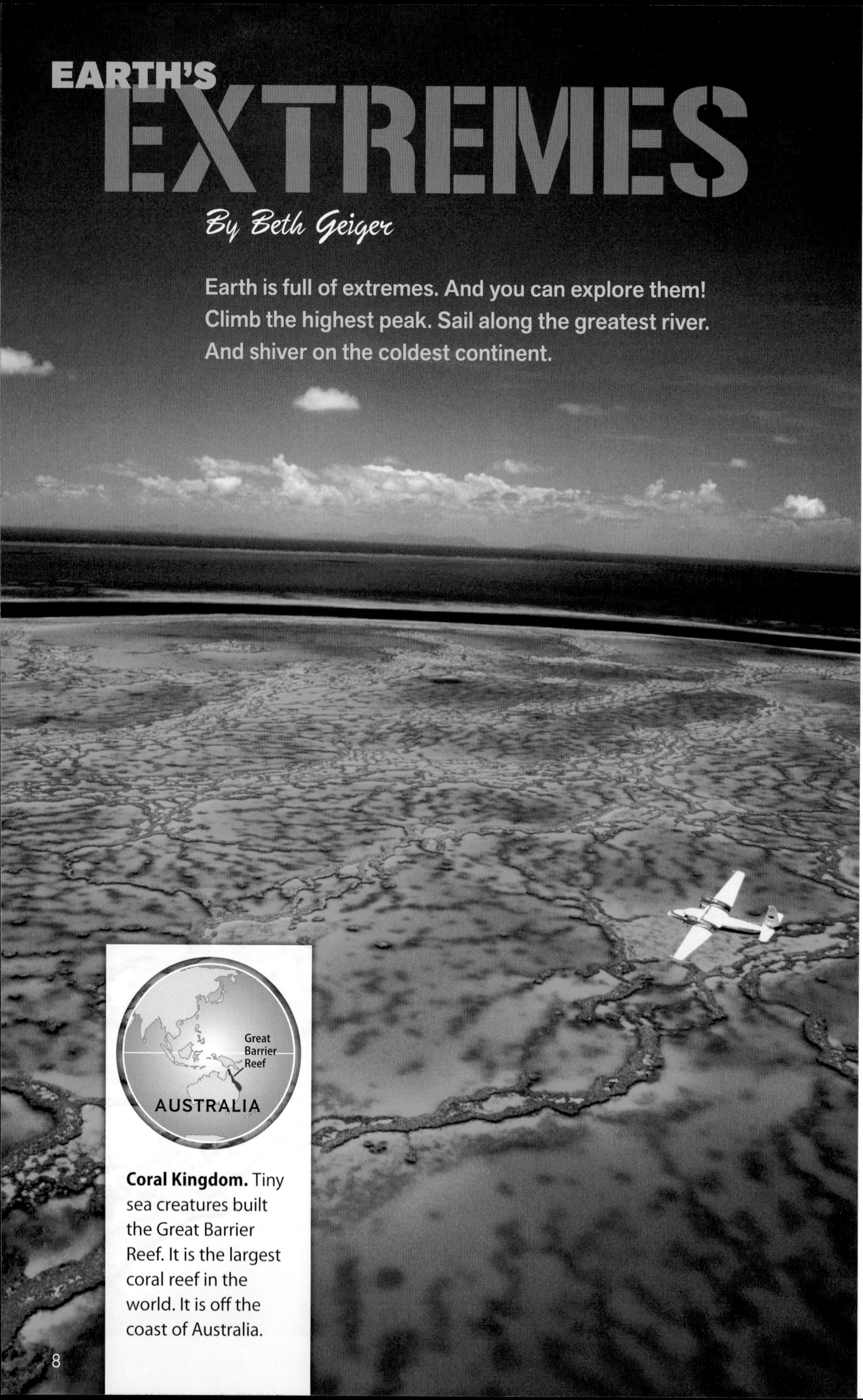

Coral Kingdom. Tiny sea creatures built the Great Barrier Reef. It is the largest coral reef in the world. It is off the coast of Australia.

Enormous Everest. No mountain is taller than Mount Everest. It is on the border of China and Nepal. The top is 8,850 meters (29,035 feet) high.

Sizzling Sands. The Sahara is the largest hot desert on Earth. It stretches across northern Africa. It is about the size of the United States. Some parts get no rain for years.

Coldest Continent. Thick ice covers Antarctica. It is at the South Pole. It stays below freezing there, even in the summer!

The Grandest Canyon. The Grand Canyon was formed by the Colorado River. It is in northwestern Arizona. The canyon is 446 kilometers (227 miles) long.

Fantastic Falls. Angel Falls is Earth's tallest waterfall. It is in Venezuela. Water drops 970 meters (3,212 feet).

Awesome Amazon. The Amazon River is the world's largest river. It runs east across Brazil. The world's largest rain forest is around the river.

AROUND EARTH

Explore Earth's most extreme places. Then answer these questions.

1. Where does the Four Deserts Race take place?
2. What are deserts like?
3. How are the four deserts different?
4. What do the photos on pages 4–7 show about each desert?
5. How are deserts like Earth's other extreme places. How are they different?